DRAMA, RUMORS, & SECRETS

staying true to yourself in changing times

by Nancy Holyoke
illustrated by Brigette Barrager

Published by American Girl Publishing

No part of this book may be used or reproduced in any manner whatsoever without written permission except in the case of brief quotations embodied in critical articles and reviews.

24 25 26 27 28 29 30 QP 10 9 8 7 6 5 4 3 2 1

Editorial Development: Darcie Johnston and Jodi Goldberg
Art Direction and Design: Gretchen Becker, Kristi Lively, Lisa Wilber
Illustrations: Brigette Barrager
Production: Jeannette Bailey, Judith Lary, Jodi Knueppel, Tami Heinz
Consultant: Jane Annunziata, Psy.D.

Library of Congress Cataloging-in-Publication Data
Holyoke, Nancy.
Drama, rumors, & secrets: staying true to yourself in changing times / by Nancy Holyoke; illustrated by Brigette Barrager.
  pages   cm. — (A smart girl's guide)
  ISBN 978-1-68337-234-9 (pbk.)
1. Girls—United States—Psychology—Juvenile literature. 2. Interpersonal relations in children—United States—Juvenile literature. 3. Interpersonal relations in adolescence—United States—Juvenile literature. 4. Social interaction in children—United States. 5. Social interaction in adolescence—United States. I. Barrager, Brigette, illustrator. II. Title.
  HQ777.H637 2015   305.230820973—dc23   2014024148

© 2015, 2018, 2025 American Girl. American Girl and associated trademarks are owned by American Girl, LLC. American Girl ainsi que les marques et designs y afférents appartiennent à American Girl, LLC. MADE IN CHINA. FABRIQUÉ EN CHINE. Retain this address for future reference: American Girl, 333 Continental Blvd., El Segundo, CA 90245, U.S.A. Conserver ces informations pour s'y référer en cas de besoin. American Girl Canada, 333 Continental Blvd., El Segundo, CA 90245, U.S.A. Manufactured, imported or distributed by: Mattel Europa B.V., Gondel 1, 1186 MJ Amstelveen, Nederland. Mattel U.K. Limited, The Porter Building, 1 Brunel Way, Slough SL1 1FQ, UK.

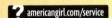
americangirl.com/service

Not all services are available in all countries.

MO

Dear Reader,

In the following pages, girls like you speak out about feuds, gossip, jealousy, competition, teasing, backstabbing, and exclusion—problems that are familiar to just about every girl between the ages of seven and seventeen.

Some girls seem to thrive on the drama these problems create. Others suffer badly. Many feel swept along by situations that bring out the worst in just about everybody. Friends turn on friends in unkind ways. People get bullied. Even kids on the sidelines are stressed out. Emotions run high, and common sense runs low.

This book shows you how to identify such hurtful situations, and how to deal with them in healthy ways. It explores why these dramas exist, how they start, what keeps them going, and how to cool them down. Along the way, you'll find quizzes to help you see how troubles develop between friends, and even how you might be contributing to them yourself. How can you avoid getting involved in a crisis? How can you handle a dramatic friend? What can you do to protect yourself? That's all here, too.

By the final pages, you'll be better able to calm down when emotions run high—and help your friends cool down, too. After all, you might not even remember most of these dramas in a few days, but friendships can last your whole life long.

Your friends at American Girl

contents

feelings rule 6
emotional overload
tears and fears
experiments
what drama means for you
rewrite the script

among friends 18
a friendly face
your friends and you
friendship truths
roles in a drama
behind the scenes
drama in action
Quiz: do you love drama?
rewrite the script

angry & annoyed 36
Quiz: what do you do when you're mad?
being in a fight
friendship fix-up
calm it down
hard stuff
rewrite the script

rumors, secrets, & screens 52

- talk vs. gossip
- words on a screen
- Quiz: you and your devices
- rumors
- Quiz: rules of the road
- getting screen savvy
- secrets
- rewrite the script

bullying 72

- Quiz: training your brain
- getting ugly
- how bullying happens
- making a difference
- when you're bullied
- getting help
- forgiveness

rewrite the script 88

- Quiz: casting call
- a fresh start

feelings rule

emotional overload

Uh-oh.

Emma's in tears because Grace and Anna were whispering together on the bus.

Katie sent a mean text to Maya from Liam's phone. Maya yelled at him in the hall.

Ava sat next to Aaliyah again at lunch. Wait till Lila finds out!

Min-ju is still mad at Jasmine because of the video she posted last week.

Three hours after Bianca broke up with Jason, Rachel was talking with him at the bus stop. Now all the soccer girls are saying mean stuff about Rachel online.

Olivia is talking a mile a minute. Is she happy? Is she mad? You don't know. But she's excited, that's for sure.

What's going on here?

It seems like everyone's always excited about something. A problem that starts between two people suddenly involves five. Then twenty. One crisis dies down and the next one starts. There are days you'd rather stay in bed with the cat than get up and deal with it all.

People use the word "drama" to describe making a big deal out of something small and silly. But no conflict seems small when you're dragged into it. Drama can change how friends treat friends. It can change how you feel about yourself. The fact is, living with daily drama is a very big deal indeed.

tears and fears

I hate puberty! I've got so many emotions and I can't control them. I feel like my world is falling apart. Help!
—Kidnapped by Puberty

You're not alone! Most kids feel torn up by emotions during puberty, and science says there's a very good reason for that.

In puberty, a girl's body produces chemicals called hormones. These hormones create physical changes that are easy to see, like growing taller and getting curvier. What you don't see is that those same hormones are also at work on your emotions. The structure of your brain is changing. The way your nervous system works is changing. These emotional changes are not as obvious as the physical ones, but they are every bit as real.

chemical changes inside the body =

Intense Emotions and MOOD SWINGS

With all these changes happening at once, a girl can feel pretty confused. Chances are, you've never been so aware of your body in your entire life—or so worried about how others see you. You compare yourself with your friends. You might compare yourself with stars on social media. Lots of girls become their own worst critics.

Getting ready in the morning used to take you five minutes. Now your dad has to knock on the bathroom door to get you away from the mirror. You may have days when you walk around all day afraid of the moment someone points a finger at a flaw you're trying to hide. School feels different. You don't want to stick out. You try hard not to make mistakes and to save face when you do.

Along the way, you may start feeling like "you" is just a part you're playing. You're changing so fast. Who can tell who you are anymore, anyway?

experiments

Who are you? How do you fit in? Who do you want to be? Now that your body is reinventing itself, you may think it's a great chance to reinvent yourself in other ways, too.

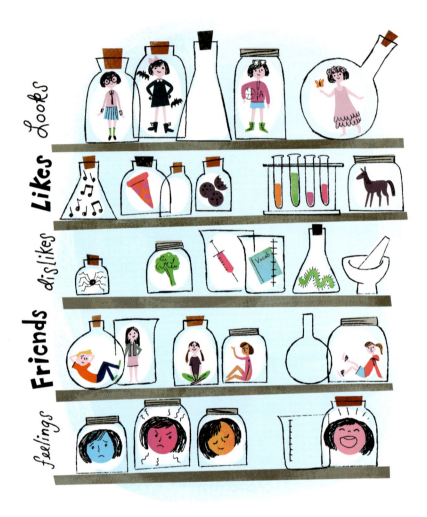

In some ways, it's all a big experiment. Does this shirt seem like you? What music do you want to hear? Do you really want to move up in soccer, or would you rather switch it up and play more tennis? A few years ago, your parents would have made a lot of these decisions. Now many of them are up to you.

You are also exploring those big, new emotions knocking around in your chest. Why can't you stop thinking about that kid you have a crush on? Why did that group chat have you crying in the bathroom over lunch? You're not quite sure.

The fact is, everybody around you is struggling with the same feelings and changes that you are. Friendships are shifting constantly, and you're all keeping track of the results.

Is Chloe getting popular? Is Maddy into hockey? Is Leah sitting with the nerds? And what about you? Do you want to hang out with your new pals from band or the friends you've had since second grade? Do you feel closer to Maria or to Layla? And does Layla feel closer to you or to Kate?

School is harder. Activities are intense. Put it in a pot and turn the heat on high. What do you get?

what drama means for you

Living in constant crisis asks all you can give and then some.

Waste of time

The trouble between Zoey and Aria has been going on for three days straight. It's a full-time job keeping up. You finally managed to settle down to work on your presentation, but every time you get an idea another text pings in.

Your friends' quarrel is eating up your life. You're getting less sleep at night and less done during the day, and the emotional ups and downs can be exhausting. You could be learning to dance, working at a soup kitchen, or biking around the lake. Instead you're caught up in a problem that you can't really do much about and that doesn't directly involve you.

Black-and-white?

Yesterday, you told Jaycee your secret. Now she's told it to Taylor. Jaycee has ruined your life.

Strong feelings—feelings like anger, fear, and sadness—can be so overwhelming that the world looks black-and-white. People and events seem either very, very right or very, very wrong. But in real life not every problem is a catastrophe, and a friend who's made a mistake isn't terrible (you make mistakes, too!). When you have a problem with a friend, you need to think and plan in order to fix it. Does overreacting help? Just the opposite.

Drama = more drama

One minute you're upset with your friend Ashley. The next you're grounded for yelling at your little sister. Your brother calls you Hurricane Hannah, and in your heart of hearts you do feel sort of like a disaster.

Moods are hard to shake. If you're mad, hurt, and anxious at school, chances are you're going to be mad, hurt, and anxious when you walk in the door at home. Problems with friends can create problems at home, and problems at home can create problems with friends.

Less trust

Last month, Sophia decided she didn't like Amber and said you should stop liking Amber, too. Today Sophia said a bunch of bad stuff about Saskia. What if Sophia decides to stop liking Saskia?

Excluding kids hurts the person who's left out, but that's not all it does. In instances like this, a single girl can poison an entire friend group by creating an atmosphere of fear and shame. Friends who should be open and free with one another get guarded. There's more plotting and planning. There's less trust. There's less truth. What you share becomes the exact opposite of what we all want from the word "friendship."

Lonely

When you're with your friends, you feel fake.

It's natural for a girl to try on different clothes, different ideas, and different ways of expressing herself. There's a little bit of acting mixed up with that, which is perfectly natural, too. It's about discovering who you are and what kind of person you want to become. The problem is that many girls are nervous about what other people think. When emotions run high, they might end up worrying more about how they *appear* than how they truly *are* and what they truly feel. That can make a person feel empty—and lonely, even among friends.

rewrite the script

People may think drama is inevitable. It isn't.
Girls like you can rewrite the script.

I don't need a lot of drama.
I can make different choices.
I can rewrite the script.

I know that other kids are like me.
Everybody wants to fit in some-
where. Everybody's trying hard to
be liked and to figure out what sort
of person she wants to be.

It's best to be fair. I don't
want to overreact or
exaggerate. When I'm
upset about something,
I try to calm down
before I act.

I'm going to try new things, but I'll decide for myself what works best for me. I'm not going to change to suit someone else.

I have strong feelings, just like most kids. My feelings aren't good or bad. They just are. I feel them. I'm not going to pretend I don't. But I will work to control them. I don't want them to control me.

I believe in doing what's right. I'm going to make some mistakes. Everybody does. But I will never stop trying to be a decent person. I'm going to grow up liking myself.

among friends

Me and my friends try to be accepting. We just like to be with each other. We help each other out and don't let rifts get in the way of being friends. We are who we are, and we're fine with that.

—MT

a friendly face

You walk into the lunchroom and look for a friendly face. It might be someone who plays on your basketball team, or sits next to you in lit group, or plays flute like you do. Whether you have several good friends or just one, it's comforting to be together. Your friends listen when you talk. They care how you feel. You can hang out and be goofy together.

> I have absolutely the most gorgeous, nice, caring friends in the world. I can trust them, and they can trust me.
> —Isabel

Our friendship is like a triple-knotted shoelace. Not even the strongest person can untie it.
—Madeline and Gabrielle

My friends and I never stay in a fight for long, and eventually we walk off happy. That's how I know we are true friends.
—Abigail

I've found friends who are 100% sincerely nice and who like me for who I am.
—Julia

your friends and you

It's natural to like the things your friends like. If a friend wears daisy clogs, you may decide to start wearing daisy clogs, too. If a friend has pierced ears, you may want to pierce your ears, too. That's OK, as long as you really want to wear daisy clogs and have your ears pierced.

But what if you don't?

What if your friends decide to wear black, and you show up in yellow plaid?

If you stop listening to country and start liking indie?

If you start spending time with someone new?

welcome ALL friends

To some girls, friendship doesn't involve a lot of dos and don'ts. They don't spend time examining what their friends wear or do or say. They don't question someone's loyalty. They also aren't hung up on disliking other kids or excluding people. They like to have different people around them and value what everyone has to say.

YOU should be like us

But other girls can be really critical. They tell their friends how to dress and what to think, who's OK to talk to and who isn't. There's always a right way and a wrong way, and they'll tell you which is which. With friends like that, a girl may feel she's always one step away from being on the outs herself.

If that describes you, it's time to remind yourself just what friendship is all about.

friendship truths

When it comes to friends, keep these truths in mind.

1. Friendship can only be given. No one can demand it from you, and you can't demand it from someone else. Every girl decides for herself who she wants to be friends with.

2. Part of being a good friend is being happy when your friends are having fun with other people. Friends need freedom. If you are too possessive—if you hold on to a friend too tight—sooner or later she'll resent it.

3. Friends aren't for ranking. You'll be happier if you think of your friends as a circle of people—not a list of your preferences, where everybody's ranked 1, 2, 3, and on down the line. Being less exclusive gives you more friends. It gives you healthier friendships. And when the day comes that you lose an important friend, you'll have others to turn to.

4. Calling somebody your friend doesn't make it true. Friendships are rooted in honesty and trust. You can't get a good friend—or be one—just by trading necklaces or dressing alike.

5. Friendships grow and change, just as you do. Sometimes you and a friend might drift apart so slowly that the two of you hardly notice it's happening. Other times, a friendship just begins to feel wrong. Maybe you're always anxious because a friend is so demanding. Or maybe you just don't enjoy a girl's company that much anymore. Either way, in cases like these it's time to find a kind way to let that friendship go.

6. That said, a great friendship never dies completely. You may be surprised. For instance, you and your BFF from third grade may have really different interests now. You like each other fine, but you're closer to other people. Friendship over? Maybe not. Come high school, you two could end up in the same play or the same science class, and hit it off all over again. Good feelings and good memories last.

roles in a drama

Imagine a friendship drama playing out onstage. There are lots of parts and lots of players. What roles look familiar to you?

1. When there's friendship drama, this girl spreads the news. She talks to everybody. Then she talks to everybody again. And again. Everyone's excited, and she's in the middle of it.

2. This girl can be found alongside the most popular kid in school. Her friend runs the show, and she gets to help. She's a sidekick, a number two. Her popular pal gives the orders, and she carries them out.

3. This girl wants to fit in. She wears what everyone else is wearing, does what they do, and says what they say. Sometimes following along makes her feel untrue to herself, but she does it anyway.

4. This girl collects information. When she wants a little excitement, she drops a secret here, a rumor there. Before long, people are all riled up, and nobody has noticed that she's the one pulling the strings.

5. This girl looks great, acts nice, and kids compete to be her friend. People do pretty much whatever she says. If someone doesn't—well, that girl might not be her friend for long.

6. This girl is hurting. Her friends make fun of her. They often exclude her. And what does she do? Nothing. If she complained, she thinks, she wouldn't have any friends at all.

behind the scenes

There are some serious drawbacks to playing these various roles.

Girl 1 Dramas feed on gossip. Being "in the know" can make a girl feel important. But a lot of bad information gets shoveled around when emotions are high. All that makes small problems bigger, and a girl who's spreading rumors will end up hurting other people.

Girl 2 Being a powerful kid's sidekick gives this girl some influence. But her identity is so tied up in pleasing her bestie, she's isolated from everyone else. Not fun.

Girl 3 This girl knows how to keep her head down, blend in, and keep up a good appearance. This protects her from a lot of bad drama, but it doesn't help her form rich relationships or feel good inside.

Girl 4 Manipulating others makes this girl a poor friend. The day will come when people realize what she's doing, and that's the day they'll stop trusting her.

Girl 5 This girl runs the show, which is what she wants, in theory. But staying on top is hard. Power she has. True friends? Not so much. Kids fear her more than like her. She may well feel as anxious and worn out as the kids who seek her approval.

Girl 6 This girl has decided there's nothing she can do to change her situation. It's not true! She can decide for herself what role she cares to play with her friends—and what roles she doesn't. She can make different choices.

other choices

There are lots of parts you can play with your friends that allow you to act freely. Here are a few of them. Do you know anyone who plays these roles? Do you?

the free agent
She has all kinds of different friends—she doesn't define herself as belonging to a single group. People see that she's independent, and they respect that.

the voice of reason
She's calm. When emotions run high, other girls come to her. She helps them cool down, focus, and fix problems. She doesn't tell anybody what to think or how to feel. She makes suggestions, but she doesn't position herself between the people who are having trouble. Her motto is, "Don't make it bigger."

the plain speaker
She says what she thinks. She doesn't make a big deal out of it. She just doesn't choose her words to please other people. It's not always been easy to do, but she's made it a goal. With practice, plain speaking has become a habit. Now she's able to handle tough situations the way she handles easy ones: with honesty.

drama in action

Drama between friends takes many forms.

Zombies

It's been a month since the field trip, but your friends are still analyzing every move Kara and Seth made that day. There is absolutely nothing new to say—nada, zip—but everyone keeps talking about it anyway. You're like zombies! *Must talk about Kara and Seth, must talk about Kara and Seth…*

Some dramas refuse to die. When you and your friends are stuck in one, you may feel like it's eating away at your brain tissue. It's the same old stuff, over and over again—none of it solving anything and all of it going nowhere. It's beyond boring. What to do? Just say: "OK guys, let's change the subject."

Not a game

Wren is in a fight with Hallie. Every day you pump her for the latest and tell her what to do. Then she does it. It's like one of those games that require a lot of strategy. There are so many people involved by now, it's super complicated and (to be honest) super fun.

Giving advice can be an act of friendship. Entertaining yourself with a friend's dilemma is not. Wren is a person, not a game piece. She needs to solve her own problems, and you need to step back from the drama and let her do it.

Switcheroo

Caitlin has always been your best friend. She still is, sort of—only not when she's with her other friends. If she's with them, she does a big switcheroo and pretends you don't exist.

It's hard to know what's going on with a friend like this. She may be temporarily caught up in some unhappy role with these other girls. She may be exploring new relationships, experimenting with a new sense of who she is or might want to be. But this much is clear: She's treating you poorly. So find a private moment and tell her how you feel and how you'd like things to change ("I feel hurt when you don't even say hi in the halls. If we're friends, we should be able to talk, no matter who's around"). How she responds will tell you whether she wants to keep the friendship alive or not. Either way, now's a good time for you to grow other friendships. Caitlin is changing, and you'll need to change, too.

Good drama

Reagen posted something ugly about your friend Shawna. You go up to Reagen in the lunch line and say, "What you said about Shawna isn't true. You should take it down and apologize to her." Never, ever was the lunchroom so quiet. For once, Reagen doesn't have a comeback. By the time you get back to your seat, the news is all over school.

Some dramas are good, and this is one of them. You stood up for a friend against a powerful girl. It was brave. Kids are talking about you because they know that. You did the right thing, and that sent a bolt of joy through every kid who's been intimidated by someone like Reagen. If people are talking about this next week (which they will be), that's great. The best stories have heroes, and in this story the hero is you.

Quiz

do you love drama?

What sounds like you? What doesn't?

1. Bailey walks in with a new purse. "What are you doing with my grandma's purse?" you say. Everybody laughs. You keep going all night with the purse jokes. You love making your friends laugh. Maybe you'll be on TV when you grow up.

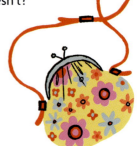

me   not me

2. Scarlett and Sofia are hanging out at your place. Why aren't you having fun? Because you're all watching a drama blow up on your phones, that's why. You say, "OK guys. Let's turn off our phones and do wacky hairstyles!"

me   not me

3. What a day! You've been texting nonstop. First Silas dropped Abby. Then Fernanda was flirting with Joel. The war between Alli and Shetara exploded online. AND something totally embarrassing happened to Avery, which you'd be telling Missy about right now, but the battery on your phone died.

me   not me

4. It's midnight at the slumber party. "OK. We all have to share one secret—to show we're really friends," says Shoshana. You recognize this for what it is: a recipe for disaster. "Nah," you say. "How about everybody pick a favorite movie, and then we watch one."

me   not me

5. Last week, you and Aubrie got in a fight. She apologized, but you are still talking about how hurt you were. "Maybe you should just let it go," a friend suggests wearily. What?! Let it go?!?! You are sooooooo hurt that she would say that!

me   not me

6. Katie says, "Pedro really likes you, Skylar. You should send him a cute video of yourself." You know that Pedro has told Katie no such thing. You say, "Don't do it, Skylar."

me   not me

Answers

The more **odd numbers** you said "me" to, the more you love drama. You love being center stage, having an audience, and expressing yourself. You don't react small—you react BIG. You like to make things exciting. You like a world full of exclamation points!!!!!!!!!!!!!! It's more fun! Boo on boredom!!!

But stop for a moment and think about how this looks from where your friends sit. You'll make fun of a friend if it lets you shine. You'll make others uncomfortable to entertain yourself. While you're lost in the excitement of the moment, your friends are likely feeling hurt, annoyed, and just plain exhausted.

If you identify more with the **even numbers,** drama's not for you. You prefer having fun to obsessing over your phone. You also know how to solve problems and shut down a drama before it starts. Your friends will like you more for your easy ways and common sense. And when your head hits the pillow at the end of the day, you'll like yourself more, too.

rewrite the script

People may think drama is inevitable. It isn't.
Girls like you can rewrite the script.

I can be friends with anyone
I want to be friends with.

Being friends doesn't mean being
the same—or thinking the same.
I'm not going to criticize my
friends for being different, and I'm
going to expect them to accept me
in the same way.

Friendships should be
about inviting people in,
not keeping people out.

Friendship shouldn't be a power struggle. I'm not going to set rules for my friends to follow, and if they try to set rules with me, I'll ask them to stop.

My friends aren't rungs on a ladder. I'm going to make friends with the people who make my heart sing—not the people who will make me more popular.

I love my friends, and I care what they think. But they don't decide what I do. I'm responsible for my own choices.

angry & annoyed

When my friend gets mad, she won't talk to me and keeps on giving me the stink eye. Then the next day she acts all nice, like nothing happened.
—Erin

The drama I face happens when my friends and I don't choose our words carefully. Sometimes we say mean things that we don't really mean.
—Amanda

Quiz

what do you do when you're mad?

Which sounds most like you?

1. Ever since Emma started liking Samuel, you've felt second best. You . . .

   a. tell Emma, "You're getting stuck-up."

   b. tell Emma you feel sad and ignored, and would like to spend more time with her.

   c. say nothing—and get madder every day.

   d. invite five other girls over on Saturday and leave Emma out.

2. Moira told Thu that you like Gabe. Argh! You . . .

   a. tell Moira she's an awful person.

   b. tell Moira you're upset and you expect her to keep your secrets better in the future.

   c. ignore it. If you got mad, Moira would just get mad back.

   d. tell every kid in science that Moira likes Evan.

3. Jada gave your BFF Brianna a friendship bracelet. Grr! You . . .

  a. tell Jada she's nobody and Brianna likes you better.

  b. tell your big sister you feel jealous of Jada and get some advice about what you can do to feel better.

  c. are super nice to Jada so she won't know you hate her.

  d. tell Brianna that Jada has been saying mean things about her.

4. Yesterday, your little sister sang her donkey song for you and Rose. Now Rose is making fun of her. You . . .

  a. call Rose a name and tell her to shut up.

  b. say, "My sister loves that song. Don't make fun of her. It's mean, and it hurts my feelings."

  c. do nothing. If you pretend it's not happening, maybe Rose will stop.

  d. tell everyone how Rose bombed the Spanish test.

5. You lent your favorite sweater to Dominique. You've asked for it back three times. Today she walks in and says, "Oopsie! Sorry. Forgot!" You . . .

  a. say, "So, are you just stealing my sweater or what?"

  b. say, "I've asked you to give my sweater back three times. It's upsetting. I really want it back. When can I stop by your house to pick it up?"

  c. say, "No problem." It wouldn't be nice to get mad.

  d. give her the silent treatment all day. When she asks what's wrong, you say, "Nothing."

Answers

People deal with anger in lots of different ways.

If you checked **mostly a's,** you blow your top. When you're mad or hurt, you lash out. Your friends get punished before they have a chance to change course or apologize. Sometimes they may not even be sure why you're mad. You never actually stop and tell them what the problem is. Next time, try hitting "pause" before you react. Look for words that explain instead of words that wound. That's what will help make a bad situation better.

If you checked **mostly b's,** you try to fix the problem. When you're mad or hurt, you say so, and you find a good way to say it, too. Your friends know why you're upset with them, and what you want them to do next. All this keeps the air clear, cuts down the drama, and leaves you feeling lighter for having said what you think.

If you checked **mostly c's,** you absorb the hurt. You think that getting mad is bad—that if you admit to being upset, you're not being "nice." It's just not true. A girl can express hurt and anger in ways her friends can respond to and respect. If you don't learn to do that, your anger is going to burn you up inside. You'll like yourself less, and your problems will be going nowhere.

If you checked **mostly d's,** you attack— but indirectly. If you're mad at a girl, you may exclude her, embarrass her, undermine her friendships, or hurt her reputation. Or you may just mess with her mind by freezing her out. The one thing you don't do is admit you're mad. You hurt your friends, lose their trust, and gain nothing. You don't even get to say what you're really feeling.

being in a fight

A lot of girls have trouble saying "I'm mad" or "I'm hurt." Instead, they send out the message in a hundred other ways.

Whoa! This girl is NOT feeling friendly.
What's up? What's the problem?

You know how it works:

A girl can send hostile signals with how she stands, looks, and sits.
She can leave a friend out and pretend she didn't mean to.
She can stir up trouble with gossip and rumors.
She can make fun of a friend . . .

Just kidding!

and deny that it's hurtful.

Can't you take a joke?

She can make a friend question her own feelings . . .

You're so sensitive.

and her own judgment.

No, I didn't. You just imagined it.

When a girl denies what she's doing, it can drive a friend crazy.

Am I imagining it?

Am I being too sensitive?

This feels all wrong, but maybe it's my fault!

Did that just happen?

If I apologize, will this stop?

So why do girls express anger in this indirect way?

It's easier—and safer.

A girl doesn't have to explain what her problem is.

She doesn't have to have a big, scary discussion, which she can't control.

She can get other girls to side with her, because they hear only her version of things.

Other people won't think she's mean, because she can always deny what she's doing.

Is this the best way to solve a problem?

No! It doesn't solve the problem at all. Freezing out a friend tells her that you're mad. It can make her suffer. It can make her surrender. But what it does NOT do is acknowledge the situation that made one girl so mad to begin with. To do that, you need to communicate openly. You need to talk.

friendship fix-up

Something happened. Now you're unhappy with a friend. What do you do?

Name your feelings.

You're upset. What exactly are your feelings about? Are you mad? Sad? Hurt? Scared? Ashamed? Stop and figure out exactly what's going on inside you and why you're feeling that way.

Get the words right.

Get everything that's happened clear in your head. Write it down if that helps. Be specific. What did you see and hear? How did you feel? Avoid words that accuse and words like "always" and "never." Push yourself to stick with the facts.

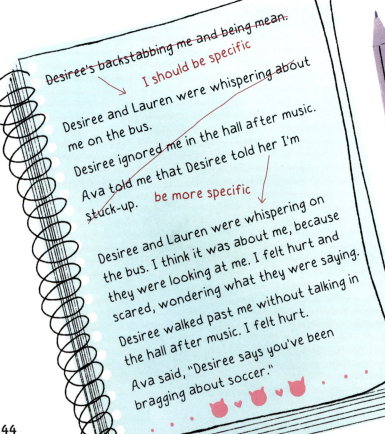

~~Desiree's backstabbing me and being mean.~~ *I should be specific*

Desiree and Lauren were whispering about me on the bus.

Desiree ignored me in the hall after music.

Ava told me that Desiree told her I'm stuck-up. *be more specific*

Desiree and Lauren were whispering on the bus. I think it was about me, because they were looking at me. I felt hurt and scared, wondering what they were saying.

Desiree walked past me without talking in the hall after music. I felt hurt.

Ava said, "Desiree says you've been bragging about soccer."

Practice.
You'll have to talk to this girl. Is that scary? Maybe. But it's the only way to set things right. So look into the mirror and practice using your "right words." Practicing will make you better at saying what you have to say and give you confidence.

Explain.
Find a private time to approach your friend, when you can talk face-to-face. (This is definitely not the time to text.) Tell her what you think has happened and how you feel about it. Be sure she knows you're interested in solving the problem, not in attacking her.

Hear your friend out.
Ask her what she thinks. Then listen. And don't correct her—no matter how much you want to. She has to have her say, too. Remember that your friend hasn't been practicing like you have, so it may take a while for her to find her own "right words."

Be patient.
Give yourselves some time, and see if you can find things to agree on.

You: When you're with Lauren, I feel like you're against me.

Desiree: We're not against you. Honest.

You: Lauren is cool, but I don't feel as close to her as I do to you.

Desiree: I know it's been different lately. I wish we had more classes together.

Desiree: I'm sorry we were talking about you.

You: I'm sorry I got jealous.

Desiree: You really *did* win the last soccer game for us.

calm it down

A drama can suck up every kid within miles. What do you do when you feel yourself getting pulled in? Here are some simple things that help a lot.

Do things you love.
What do you love to do? It could be water ballet, soccer, tae kwon do, theater, drawing, science club, dancing, writing, singing, kayaking, skateboarding, or tennis. Whatever it is, if it makes you happy, now's the time to get out there and do it. Connect with new people. Be creative. Run hard and feel your heart beat. If you don't have a big passion, that's OK. You can still sign up for a team, take classes in something fun, or join a club. It will keep your brain and body active, lighten your mood, and give you skills you can be proud of.

Have some friends outside of school.
Chances are, you know some nice girls outside of school. Stop and think who they are: That girl in choir? Your old friend who ended up at a different school? Ariana from gymnastics? Your cousin Julie? Try to build up some of these friendships. For one thing, it'll be fun. For another, it gives you a friend or two who's not part of the daily drama. That's fresh air and blue skies on days when other friends are upset.

Help others.

Step outside the door and volunteer. Tutor younger kids in math. Read to elderly people in a nursing home. Sort clothes with your mom at the local thrift shop. Take care of abandoned animals at a local shelter. Guaranteed: Your world will get bigger, and your own problems will seem smaller.

Get some advice.

There are times it's nice to have an older girl to talk to. It could be a sister, a favorite aunt, a cousin, or a high-school girl from down the block. Look around for someone you like and trust—a person you can go to for advice. She will have been through what you're going through now and come out the other side. Think of her as your future self! You'll be that wiser, older girl yourself soon.

Today isn't forever.

When things are bad, today feels like forever—that's for sure. But today is not forever. It's not, it's not, it's not. Things change over time. Keep telling yourself that. Time helps.

hard stuff

Dealing with upset feelings is never easy.

A big deal

Paula calls you every day for help in math. She doesn't even bother to read the book! She expects you to do it for her! You don't want to make a big deal of this, so you help her, but you also start making fun of her at lunch.

Anger isn't like water. You can't bottle it up and expect it to stay there. Anger wants to come out. If you don't express it directly, you'll express it indirectly—whether you plan on doing it or not. So say the true thing: "Paula, we're friends, and friends help each other. But I feel like you're always asking me for answers that are right there in the book. I can help you, but I can't do your work for you." Paula may be upset at first, but if you express yourself kindly, chances are she'll change, and your friendship will be better for it. As it is, you're overworked. You're mad inside. You're doing things that hurt your friend—and she has no clue why. Isn't that a big deal, too?

Saving face?

Clara has tears in her eyes. She's so mad she's shaking. You know you're in the wrong, but if you admit what you did, everybody will hate you. You have to fight back!

It's scary. OK...it's *really* scary to be face-to-face with someone you know has good reason to be mad at you. But what you really have to do is admit your mistake. It's what being a decent person is all about. If you try to save face, the whole mess will just keep going, and you'll still be trying to save face three months from now. Put a stop to it now! Be brave. Say what you did and say you're sorry.

Eating gravel

Olivia didn't always make fun of you. She used to be nice. Once in a while she still is, and you get up every morning hoping that today will be one of the good days. You can't be mad. Olivia's a really cool person, and she *is* your best friend.

You remember what it was like when Olivia was kind. You know how that felt, and you know how you feel now—miserable. You're telling yourself this is OK when you know it's not. This girl is feeding you a steady diet of gravel. It's weighing you down, making you less sure of yourself every day. The biggest danger isn't that Olivia will drop you if you demand to be treated kindly (which, by the way, you should!). The biggest danger is that you'll get used to accepting this behavior as friendship.

War!

You are so mad at Amy! You tell Breanna what she's done. You and Cybil don't say a single word to Amy on the field trip. You tell Amy's secrets to Daniella, and you start a rumor with Evan. Then you post some anonymous comments about Amy online. This is war!

Hold on a minute. You're mad. Understood. You may have very good reasons to be so. But that doesn't mean you're free to attack this girl. It doesn't mean you've got the right to be mean, violate confidences, or hurt her reputation. Anger is a feeling—not a reason for bad behavior. You need to talk to Amy directly, tell her how you feel, and explain what you want her to do to make things right. That gives you a chance to express yourself and her a chance to respond, and it's a whole lot healthier than nursing your anger in secret while stirring up trouble behind her back.

rewrite the script

Some people think drama is inevitable. It isn't.
Girls like you can rewrite the script.

Everybody gets mad sometimes. Feeling mad doesn't make me a bad person. It doesn't make my friends bad, either.

All people disagree sometimes. Talking through a disagreement can help solve problems that would get bigger if they're ignored.

I can disagree with my friends in a way that respects both them and me.

When I'm mad or hurt, I'm going to say so. I'm not going to deny it and then go do something hurtful behind the other person's back.

I can admit when I'm wrong. It's scary, but I'll do it.

When two people have a problem, they have to solve it face-to-face—not working through other kids. I am strong enough to do that.

rumors, secrets, & screens

> People say things online that they won't say in person.
> —AG Fan

> People think technology is a game, and you can do and say anything you want. But what you say online can hurt people just as much as if you said it to their face.
> —Sarah

> If friends would just try to communicate better and not gossip, a lot of drama wouldn't happen.
> —An AG Reader

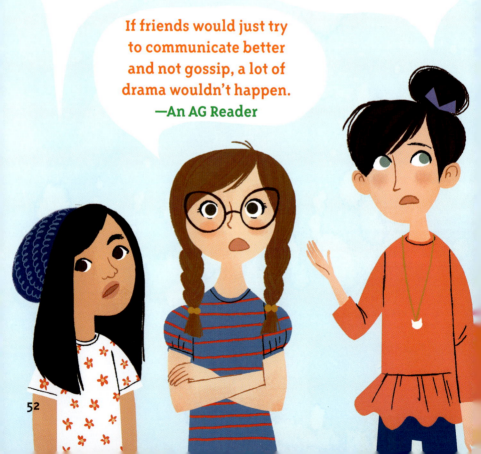

At my school, the main drama is gossip. Everybody gossips about someone different and spreads rumors about that person. One time I was the victim, and it really hurt me inside. When I saw people whispering about me, I went up to them and said, "Guys, this is not cool."
—Katie

My best friend always tells me secrets about other people. I feel bad about it, because these other people don't know what she's doing. I have to wonder whether I can trust her with MY secrets. She's my best friend, but who knows who she's telling.
—Anonymous

Girls start rumors, hear rumors, and spread rumors every day. A lot of times we don't even realize we're saying something mean— we're just talking. But rumors can make people's lives miserable and leave marks forever.
—C. in MI

talk vs. gossip

Friends talk about friends all the time. Kids talk about other kids.

It's natural. You and your friends talk about what you care about, and that includes other people. All this talking connects you. It's a big part of being friends.

What's the difference between that natural sharing and gossiping? It's not always easy to say. What one person takes as gossip, another person may defend as good communication.

Friends talk things out. So I'm talking.

I'm asking for advice.

A friend has been ignoring me, and I'm trying to figure out why.

I'm expressing how I feel.

The rumor is all over school. People are upset. Of course I'm talking about it!

I'm just saying what happened.

So how are you to judge what you can say freely and what you shouldn't?

Before you start talking—or send that text or post that comment—ask yourself these questions:

Are you talking about something another person considers private?

Would you totally change what you're saying if the person you're talking about appeared?

If this person found out what you're saying, would she feel mad or hurt? And would you feel guilty?

Are you making another kid look bad? Are you hurting her reputation? Are you damaging her friendships?

Are you saying things to make yourself more powerful or popular? Or to make someone like you?

Is this just feeding a drama?

If any answer is **yes,** it's a red flag. You're over the line. Call it "talking" or call it "gossiping"—it's hurtful.

> Honestly? I gossip. Everybody gossips. But I guess it's more fun to gossip about other people than to have people gossip about you.
> —Lily

Precisely. And that's why you should let your answers to these questions help you decide what to say—and what not to say.

words on a screen

Texts, chats, social posts, online gaming—the ways kids communicate increase every day, and that's great. Technology lets you make plans with your friends, work together on projects, post schedules, send nice messages at important (and unimportant!) moments, and share a hundred things you love to share, from photos to videos to music to a good laugh over the latest cat video.

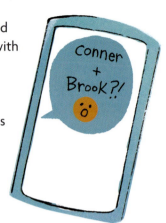

That said, talking online is very different from talking face-to-face, and those differences let gossip and drama flourish.

No faces, no clues

When you're talking face-to-face, you have all sorts of clues about what the other person is thinking. You can read a friend's feelings in her face, in her body, in her voice. She may nod her head if she agrees with what you're saying. If she's bored, her eyes may drift off to something behind you. If she's annoyed, you'll see that, too. You may change what you're saying (and how you're saying it) depending on what you see. And, of course, your friend is "reading" you at the same time. Even talking on the phone, you can get clues from the other person's voice.

But when words are going back and forth on a screen? It's a whole different deal. A smiley may help signal a mood, but there is far less to go on.

No brakes, no sympathy

When writing, you're inside your own head. *Tap, tap, tap.* Send! *Tap, tap, tap.* Post! You're in the zone, juggling words. You aren't thinking about the consequences the way you do when you're looking at a face. It's easy to get carried away. You may say too much and regret it. You may say what you mean poorly and be misunderstood. You may also get harsher—more sarcastic. It's "only a post," so you may say things you'd be too nice to say in person and may not even really believe.

No consequences

Things get ten times worse when people write anonymously. Writing anonymously gives a person the exciting sense that she can try on a whole new personality. A girl may let her emotions run without check. She no longer needs to be fair. She can say and do all kinds of things without answering for it, and she can pretend it doesn't have consequences in the real world, when of course it has big ones.

No privacy, no escape

People share, people forward, people post. Conversations go public, and problems between kids play out in front of the whole world. Kids end up on display at the worst possible moment, with nowhere to hide. If someone wants to hurt or humiliate someone else, reaching for a phone can be an easy answer. But it's not the right answer. The more upset you are, the more important it is to talk to people directly.

Respect

Devices are fun and helpful, but when you lose control of how you use them, bad things happen. People deserve respect—that's the rule. It holds true for both the virtual world and the real one.

Quiz

you and your devices

Who's running the show—you or your devices?

1. *Ping!* It's the 12th text from Zoey. You are both super upset. You ...

a. walk the dog while you cool down. Then you call Zoey to talk about it.

b. write back instantly—what else? And you do the same thing every five minutes for the next hour.

2. You write something very, very personal to Livia, which you would die if anyone else saw. For a brief moment, you remember that you don't trust Livia. You ...

a. trash the message.

b. send the message. It felt so good to write. Why waste it?

3. You're in a gaming chat with Melany. She's getting on your nerves, and a red light comes on in your brain. *Temper! Temper!* You say ...

a. "I'm tired, Melany. I'm signing off. Let's talk about this before school."

b. "WHAT'S YOUR PROBLEM? CAN YOU JUST LET IT GO FOR ONCE?"

4. Gabriel posts a super-awkward photo of you with the caption: "LOL. Just what ARE you doing here, Ellie?" You . . .

    a. ignore it.
    b. immediately write a long explanation about sticky rice noodles.

5. You're texting with Hailey. Bradon sits down and says, "Say hi from me." You say . . .

    a. "Hi from Bradon."
    b. "Bradon just landed from Planet Dork. I think he's sweet on u!!"

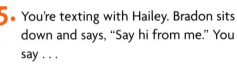

Answers

If you answered **mostly a's,** you have a healthy relationship with your devices. You know when they're helpful and when they're not. You're focused on real people, real situations, and what you really think—not on messaging.

If you answered **mostly b's,** you're operating on autopilot. You respond before you think. You message when you're anxious. You message when you're mad. You send unkind wisecracks that could cause trouble down the road. All this makes you a less appealing friend. It also makes you more vulnerable, because you end up oversharing, even when it may well cause you grief.

It's a common thing: People get so used to getting and sending messages, they don't feel normal without a phone in their hands. But sending and receiving 24/7 is not normal. It's only a habit. You can break it, and you'll have better relationships if you do. You should own your device. Don't let it own you.

rumors

Rumors don't come out of nowhere.
People create them—and the recipe is *not* appetizing.

Recipe for a Rumor
(Feeds one school for weeks)

Step 1: Select your ingredients. Find a topic (and a target). A lot of rumors start out as a problem between two people. So think: Are you in a fight with a friend? Jealous of someone? A rumor can offer revenge. You can trash the kid online. You can wreck the reputation of one person to impress somebody else. Just think up a story!

Step 2: Add gossip and stir. You want this rumor to grow. So spread the word. Send texts. Post some posts. Are there two sides to a story? Ignore them. Are important details left out? Who cares! Exaggerate the juicy parts. Don't worry about being fair or accurate. This is a rumor, after all.

Step 3: Season with emotions. Be outraged! Be shocked! Laugh at others' mistakes! React BIG! It makes the rumor seem exciting and important, even if it's small and silly.

Step 4: Beat the topic daily. Don't let it rest. A rumor never has a single cook. Repeat a rumor, and you're in the kitchen along with whoever started it.

Step 5: Cook online. If you post a bunch of nonsense after dinner, in the morning half the school may think it's true. That's the weird magic of the written word: People tend to believe it. People also tend to go with the crowd. An entire school may consider something common knowledge when there isn't an ounce of truth in it.

That sounds awful!

Awful, indeed.

But let's be honest: Rumors exist because they entertain people. A scandal can liven up a boring day. A person can also feel a bit better about herself when someone else has made a mistake. (She probably feels safer, too, when the spotlight is trained on another girl.)

Of course, if the rumor is about you, it's incredibly hurtful and often incredibly unfair. So here's what a girl should really do as far as rumors go:

Be skeptical of the facts.
Don't believe everything you hear. How does the person telling you a story know what she supposedly "knows"? Was she there when the thing happened or is she just repeating something she's heard? Why is she telling you this, anyway? What does she get out of the situation?

Be skeptical of yourself, too.
We all tend to believe what we want to believe. We also tend to believe what we fear might be true. It's human nature. Before you jump on the bandwagon, ask yourself what makes you want to help this rumor along.

And if the story is true, so what?
Say someone has made a mistake. Someone has embarrassed herself horribly. The story is true. Do you really want to be one more person who won't let her forget it? Treat this girl the way you'll want others to treat you the day you make your own embarrassing mistake.

Don't be afraid to speak up.
"That's just a rumor. I don't buy it." "Why should I believe that?" "Why are we talking about this?" "Who says?" Ask a few simple questions, and a big, important rumor can go poof and vanish before your very eyes.

Quiz

rules of the road

There are some common rules for behaving well and being safe online. Do you know them? Let's find out. What's a good move? What's not? Answer thumbs-up or thumbs-down.

1. When you write something to a friend, you consider how much you trust her and how you would feel if the message went public.

2. You don't share your passwords—except with your closest friends.

3. Jaycee's message makes you laugh so hard you've got soda coming out of your nose. If you forward it, Ethan will laugh, and Sara will ♥ you for sharing. But Jaycee might want to keep it private, so you do.

4. Anjali's upside down. Her mouth's open, her hair is a mess, and her eyes are goofy. You click. Funniest photo *EVER*. While Anjali yells, "No!" you send it to Ciara. Ciara won't share it. And anyway, Anjali's done stuff like this to you.

5. You and Cora are partners on a history project. She calls and asks, "So what are you doing right now?" The answer is that you're sitting on your bed in your PJs experimenting with a curling iron. It's not going so well. You look like a Wookie struck by lightning. You take a selfie but decide not to send.

6. Sofia sneaks Ryan's phone out of his jacket and types a message to Abby: `Hi Abby, I really like you! Ryan` "No, Sofia," you say. "Don't send that."

7. Taylor has been kicked out of the game all week by an avatar named Tricky Tiger. You know Amelia is Tricky Tiger. You say, "Amelia, what's the deal with excluding Taylor? Stop it. You should tell her it's you and apologize."

8. You want to break up with Zach. It's WAY too awkward to do it in person, so you just text him.

9. The posts in the chat are piling up. Wow. It's mean, mean stuff about Evelyn. Can what they say be true? You don't write anything, but you keep reading.

Answers

1. Don't expect privacy online. When you send something, it's out of your control. 100 percent.

2. Don't share passwords. The only people who should know your passwords are your parents. They own the accounts. Chances are, they own the devices. Their access protects you in all kinds of ways.

But sharing passwords with friends? No. Passwords aren't like a piece of jewelry that you trade to show your affection. They give people access to your whole private world: messages with your parents, messages with other friends. You aren't just violating your own privacy. You're violating the privacy of everybody who communicates with you.

Also, be practical. Friends get curious. Friends get mischievous. Friends get pressured into doing things. And friendships change. Protecting yourself online is often about setting smart limits on what you will and won't do. Keeping passwords to yourself is a big one.

3. Don't forward messages. When a friend sends a message just to you, it's been worded just for you. So respect your friend's privacy. Unless it's pure information ("Soccer practice was moved to 5:00"), don't pass a message on.

4. Don't share embarrassing pictures of other people. Friends can get silly with each other because they trust each other. That's why goofy photos exist. But share a goofy picture of a friend, and you're inviting the whole school to laugh at her.

5. Don't share embarrassing pictures of yourself, either. It's simple: If you'd be happy to see that photo of you posted on the front door at school, send it. If you wouldn't, don't.

6. Don't pretend to be someone else. Sending messages from someone else's device may seem like a harmless prank in the moment—and sometimes it probably is harmless, if everybody knows what has happened right away. But it's a joke designed to embarrass someone, it hurts trust, and it's the kind of thing that does real damage.

7. Don't exclude people. Excluding people online is as hurtful as excluding them in person—maybe even more so, because a girl like Taylor doesn't know who her enemies are, why she's being blocked, or what she's done to deserve it. She has no way to defend herself.

8. Don't fight or break up online. No one likes an awkward conversation, but life is full of them. You can't run, and you can't hide in a text. When feelings are at stake, you should talk to the other person face-to-face. This boy deserves that.

9. Don't view mean stuff. You know not to join in on mean chats, and that's good. But reading itself is a kind of participation. It rewards the kids who are posting. Without an audience, they wouldn't be doing what they're doing. Log off.

getting screen savvy

Without good digital habits, life can get pretty messy.

Reply!

A text lands from Bella. "I told Camila you didn't vote for her. Sorry! Just slipped out." Your heart flips over. Why would Bella do that? You're furious. You have no idea what you're going to say, but you hit reply.

When you're anxious or mad, every cell in your body may want to fire off a reply that very instant. Don't do it. Walk away from the screen. Set the alarm for an hour and don't go back till it rings. Take a shower. Talk to your mom. Run around the block. Shoot baskets. The extra time gives you a chance to calm down and think: *What might happen if I said this? Or that?* If there's a lot at stake, write the message, save it, and reread it in an hour. An enormous amount of drama happens because people react too fast. Slow it down.

Please, like me!

Your friend posted a picture of herself on a social site and got 17 likes. A couple kids even said she looked pretty. You take 20 selfies, pick the best one, post it, and then hold your breath, thinking, *Please, like me!*

Getting "likes" on social media says nothing about who you really are. In fact, being so concerned about what others think can make you try to be someone you're not just to get "likes." Stay true to you! And, anyway, there will always be people who aren't online to be nice or constructive—or even honest, for that matter. Whatever form that takes under your photo, it is probably not going to make you feel good. You may come away liking yourself less, and that would be too bad.

Anonymous?

Everyone at the sleepover agrees: Lauren is a total stalker and the most annoying girl at school. You spend the night posting anonymous things about her and laughing yourselves silly. In the morning, you think, *Whew. Glad no one knows who we are.*

People may not know who you are now, but they can find out. Every website can trace a post to a member if it wants to. If Lauren or her parents complain, you and your friends could be identified, and your accounts could be blocked. Depending on what else has been going on, you kids could even be charged with cyberbullying. That's serious. Will that happen? Who knows. But forget anonymous. There are no secrets at a slumber party. Word will get out regardless. People will talk. Chances are, Lauren will know who was involved before you have to look her in the eye in art class.

Very clever

You're very clever, you're very funny, and you love writing about the silly things people do. Everyone reads your Top Ten posts, and your "worst hair" poll is legendary. If certain people have a problem with you—well, they shouldn't be so sensitive.

Getting people to laugh at themselves, poking fun at pretentions— it's what the best comics do. BUT. You're not on TV, making jokes about rich and powerful people. You're in a small community called a school, writing about kids who worry all the time about being liked and accepted, and whose worst nightmare is having other kids laugh at them. So do something else with all that creative energy. Write a book or a play instead. You can make up all the characters you want, have every bit as much fun, and share your wit with every kid in the school without hurting any of them.

secrets

Sharing a secret with another girl is a way of saying, *I trust you. You're special to me. We're close.* If you're excited or troubled, it feels good to have someone to confide in. But put other friends into the mix and things can change pretty fast. Does this sound familiar?

You know a secret. That secret feels like a little gold coin in your pocket. You're special. You've got something valuable. The problem is that nobody knows you have it.

So maybe you drop a teeny-tiny hint. You want people to know that you know more than they do. You want them to know how close you are to your friend.

Now you're the center of attention. You refuse to tell. But once others know that the secret exists, they'll want to pry it out of you and will be mad if you clam up.

You want to tell. Your brain starts to whir: Maybe that coin in your pocket could buy you something here. If you tell, maybe this other girl will like you more. What's the harm, after all? She won't tell anybody. She promised. And, anyway, most people probably know already. Your friend shouldn't be so hush-hush about it.

There are two ways this can end.

1. You tell.

You give this other girl that little coin in your pocket. Is she a better friend now? No. Are you closer to her? No. You can't buy friends by betraying other friends. You haven't gained anything. But she has. She knows something that could hurt both your friend and your friendship. What will she do with it? Who knows. Whatever she likes. It's all in her hands.

How do you feel at this moment? Not happy. You're too busy dreading the moment your friend finds out what you've done.

How will she feel about you? Not good.

And what can you expect from other people when you need a friend to confide in?

Not much.

Yes. It's Chris.

I knew it!

2. You don't tell.

You may get some blowback from people who wish you would talk, but it will pass.

When the dust clears, you walk off as a girl someone can trust. You didn't do the easy thing. You didn't do the tempting thing. You did the right thing. You'll like yourself for that, and other people will like you more, too. You can look forward to deeper friendships, and you still have that bright little coin of trust in your pocket.

Sorry. I shouldn't have brought it up.

Humph. Well, OK.

That's how it works.
You get to choose.

rewrite the script

People might think drama is inevitable. It isn't.
Girls like you can rewrite the script.

I won't use gossip and rumors as weapons against other kids—in person or online.

I think before I send. I ask myself: *Is it clear? Is it fair? How will the other person feel about this? Will I be sorry I sent it?*

I'm not going to trade in secrets. My friends can trust me.

I don't overshare with friends. I keep some things private. It protects me.

Technology isn't for fights. If I have a problem with somebody, we'll talk it out in person.

My devices let me learn, work, listen, watch, see, and share. They're fun! But they don't run my life. I can turn them off and walk away.

bullying

> People always call me ugly. It gets worse every day.
> —Weeping Girl

> I go into the bathroom and cry all the time because I am abused by a really mean group of boys in my class.
> —Troubled

> My friend is being shunned because a popular girl is mad at her. She has been getting weird texts, like, "Where do you live?" One threatened to kill her pet.
> —C.C.

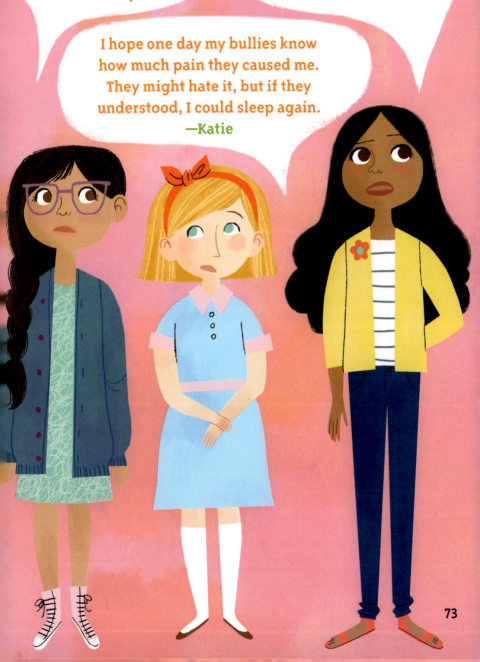

Quiz

training your brain

How people treat one another begins with how they see one another. Which answer sounds most like you?

1. Julissa never talks and seems to have no friends. Now the teacher makes you study partners. Your first reaction is: *Oh, not Julissa!* Then you . . .

a. remind yourself that you've never even talked to Julissa. Who knows what her story is? It could be interesting to find out.

b. ask the teacher to pair you with someone else.

2. The new boy in the next desk has messy hair and a worn hoodie with a teddy bear on it. Your first reaction is: *That kid is seriously weird!* Then you . . .

a. remind yourself that weird can be good. You smile at him.

b. turn away. You don't want to get connected to someone like that.

3. Magda quit talking to you the day she started sitting with Yumei. That was last year. Now Yumei is sitting with the popular kids, and Magda is sitting alone. Your first reaction is: *Serves her right.* Then you . . .

a. remember how horrible you felt when you got dumped, and invite Magda to sit with you.

b. ignore her. You hope Magda's alone the whole year.

4. Once again, Jasmine is making fun of Zuri. Your first reaction is: *I don't like what Jasmine's doing, but I don't want to make a big deal about it.* Then you . . .

   a. think about how horrible Zuri must feel and tell Jasmine to lay off.

   b. shrug. Zuri is used to it.

5. Nathan walks straight to the front, as if there weren't a line, and shoves his way in. As always. Your first reaction is: *He's the rudest, meanest kid in the entire school.* Then you . . .

   a. try to imagine why a person would act like that. Is he always this way? What's he like at home? What's he feeling inside?

   b. decide he's a horrible human being.

Answers

If you checked **mostly a's,** you've trained your brain to connect with people. You may have plenty of judgmental thoughts (we all do), but you don't go with them. When they come up, you stop. You notice what's happening. You wonder: *What would it be like to be that other person?* That gives you empathy. It means you lean toward acceptance. You lean toward understanding. It makes you more open and less fearful.

If you checked **mostly b's,** you tend to go with your first, gut reactions. If those are negative, you don't question them. You end up judging people harshly, almost without realizing you're doing it. So start noticing the dialogue going on inside your head. Ask yourself: *What am I feeling? What words are shaping my thoughts?* If they're unkind, find more generous ones. You're not covering up how you feel—you're training yourself to be more compassionate. You're training your brain to admit what you know in your deepest self to be true: that you're not so different from these other kids, and they're not so different from you.

getting ugly

As we all know, kids sometimes do mean things to one another. Why? Here are some common reasons you may hear. Let's count the good ones.

There are the reasons people say out loud.

"She deserves it. She did something bad."

"She hurt my feelings."

"She betrayed me."

"I have a right to get her back."

"We're in a fight. How else can I behave?"

There are the reasons people *don't* say out loud.

"She's stuck-up. She needs to be put in her place."

"She competes with me. She's my enemy."

"I have to do what my friends are doing."

"She scares me. She's so different."

"I want to be sure nobody thinks I'm like HER."

"I'm so unhappy. I want to make somebody else unhappy, too."

"It's fun and exciting."

"Being a little mean makes me more popular. Nobody messes with me!"

There are justifications.

"We just got a little carried away."

"She can give as good as she gets."

"I agree that people should be nice.
But this is different.
You don't understand."

There are the ways people pretend nothing is going on at all.

"It's not THAT mean."

"She's too sensitive."

"She can't take a joke."

"We were just playing around."

How many good reasons are there?

Zero.

There is no right way to be unkind to somebody else. So if you see kids trying to excuse themselves for being mean, tell them not to bother. There's nothing that turns that tar into gold.

Cruelty is wrong. Story over.

how bullying happens

Sometimes a kid is repeatedly mean to someone else in an aggressive and intentional way. There's a word for this, and that word is bullying.

What does bullying look like?

- **Excluding people**
- **Teasing**
- **Threatening others**
- **Embarrassing people**
- **Telling secrets and starting rumors**
- **Getting physical—shoving, tripping, fighting**

Who participates in bullying? The answer may surprise you. *Everyone.*

People tend to think of bullying as a drama that plays out between a "good" kid and a "bad" kid. Not so. If somebody's getting bullied by her locker, every kid in that hallway is playing a part. Those parts might include:

Kids who bully: They directly engage in hurtful behavior toward someone.

Watchers: They witness the bullying but stay silent.

Targets: They are the focus of bullying behavior.

Partners: They actively encourage the bullying and may join in.

Helpers: They might laugh or support the kid who is bullying.

Defenders: They actively defend and comfort the kid who is getting bullied.

Different kids might react in different ways on different days. But in most cases there are a whole lot of people involved who, deep down, don't like what's going on. Why do so few do anything to stop it?

Chances are, you'll hear reasons like these:

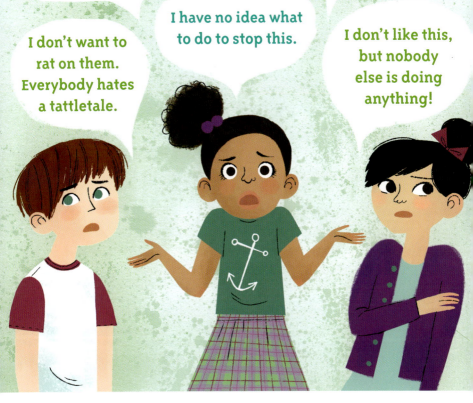

But, really, the biggest reason people don't speak up is that the community—the school and the kids in it—tolerate meanness. It's expected. It's accepted. When something ugly happens, kids don't say, "Hey, we don't do that here." It's more like, "Yeah, we've seen that. It happens."

True, you might be thinking, *but a single girl is never going to change THAT*. Maybe not completely. But a single girl can sure make a difference.

making a difference

You want to make things better. How do you start?

Take a minute to recognize your own strengths. A person who's bullying others can be intimidating. But most of the time tough talk and a rough exterior aren't signs of strength. They're signs of fear and insecurity. Real confidence comes from knowing the rules you want to live by:

I will be kind to myself and others.

I will trust my sense of right and wrong.

I will be open to all kinds of friends.

I will support others and cheer them on!

I will appreciate differences and be truly curious about them.

I will stand up for others, especially when someone is getting bullied.

Does that sound like you? Then, you got this! You don't have to be a superhero to help kids who are hurting. You can be you. And you can start small.

Opt out.

You can send a signal that you don't like what's happening. Don't laugh at the ugly joke. Don't participate in the mean conversation. Don't forward the text. Don't repeat the rumor. Pick up your books and walk off.

You're not confronting the bully directly, but this kind of resistance makes a difference. Kids look to other kids for cues. They'll think: *If she can opt out, maybe I can—and maybe I should.*

Sympathize.

You can also go up to the bullied kid later and say, "Are you OK? That was bad. I'm sorry." Your sympathy tells her she's not crazy—she really was verbally attacked, even though no one reacted. It also tells her that you know it was wrong. That can mean the world.

Use your voice.

The time may come when you feel able to speak out. Do it! You can say something short and neutral:

"Chill out."   "Ease up."   "That's enough."

You can say something stronger:

"Why are you doing this?"   "Stop it."   "This isn't right."

Are there risks? Yes. You need to think about what's safe and what's realistic. But when you speak up for kids who are being bullied, it matters. It cracks the shell of acceptance. Kids who bully want an audience and an easy victim. If they know public opinion is moving against them, it changes a lot.

Report it.

If someone is being physically threatened, or it happens repeatedly, you have to tell an adult. You have no choice. If the girl who is bullying calls you a traitor for "telling" on her, you can fairly answer: "Get real. I'm getting somebody out of trouble. If you're IN trouble, it's your own fault."

Make it the new normal.

Make a decision: You're going to be a kid who resists bullying. You're learning how, and you'll keep learning. You'll soon discover that many other kids feel the way you do. Together you can make a new normal. You don't start from, *Yeah, that happens.* You start from, *That is totally uncool and unacceptable.* Together you *can* begin to change your school.

Along the way, you will be giving hope and respect to people who profoundly need it. To them, you actually are a kind of superhero.

when you're bullied

When you're getting bullied, you may think you're the problem. You may think this is about you.

What's wrong with me?

What have I done?

How can I change?

What can I do to make them like me?

What can I do to make them stop?

But this is not about you.
It's not about anything you've done. It's not about anything you ought to be doing. It's about that other kid. This is happening because *she* wants it to. It's happening because of *her* choices. Remember that if you're ever tempted to blame yourself.

This is not about me.

There is nothing in you that needs fixing. There is nothing in you to repair. You are fine exactly the way you are. The problem lies with the kid who is bullying you. That's the person who needs to change.

82

Safety first.

There are no quick fixes here, but there is hope. For starters, avoid the places where the bullying has happened. Stay near other kids and adults you trust.

Turn away.

Walk away. Try to stay calm. Put in your earbuds or turn to a friend. Do what you can to give this hurtful person your back. Same thing if the bullying is online. Get off the site. Block the sender. Ignore the posts. Kids writing insulting things want you to respond, so they can keep the nasty talk going. Don't do it. Give them a big blank wall to work with.

Speak up.

Speaking up for yourself even a little can help. You don't have to make a big speech. A few words will do it. You might be scared, and that's OK. Make a conscious effort to stand up straight. Look the kid in the eye. It's not easy, but try anyway—and keep trying. Standing tall doesn't just make you look more confident, it helps you sound that way, too.

You should stop.

There may be times when you feel you can say more.

You: "You call me terrible names all the time. I want you to stop. I have a right to come to school without you saying cruel things to me."

Girl who bullies: "And you're going to make me?"

You: "I'm saying you're wrong to treat me like this. You should stop. I've said what I had to say. Now I'm done."

Is this going to make the bully apologize and change her ways? Probably not. But it will change you. You will have looked that girl in the eye and told her what you think. That makes you stronger.

getting help

You don't have to go through this alone. Find your helpers. Tell your parents. Tell a teacher or a counselor. A kid who is bullying you will likely mock you for "telling." In fact, you're being strong and resourceful. You need help, and you're finding it. Bullying thrives in darkness, and you're turning on the light.

Once you have some allies, you can come up with a plan together. It might go something like this:

1. Write down everything that Abby did last week.
2. Make a record of her texts and posts.
3. Go with Mom and Dad to talk to Mr. Toshibi, the principal. We'll tell him what Abby's been doing and show him the evidence.
4. We'll ask if I can have early lunch so I can eat with my friends Sarah and Til, and we'll brainstorm other ways I can have my friends around to help protect me.
5. We'll ask Mr. Toshibi to talk to Abby's parents.
6. I won't walk down hallway B after school. I won't let Abby and her friends get me alone.
7. Mom will email that one website about the posts.
8. Dad will call the cell-phone company.
9. I'll start doing gymnastics twice a week. I'll try to make new friends in math club and volunteer with Mom at the food pantry. Getting involved and spending time with kids outside school will give me other things to think about.
10. My neighbor Micah is always nice to me. Maybe she and her 10th-grade friends would talk to me about this. Older girls could have good advice!
11. If . . .

Make a detailed record.
As part of any plan, you'll need to make a record of what's been going on to help explain it to others. Write down the dates, times, and locations of important incidents. Document your digital world, too, with screenshots and printouts of bad posts and messages. A social-media website can use those things to help identify anonymous senders. Your parents can also talk to your Internet and cell-phone providers about removing posts and revoking the bully's account.

Getting adults involved may make you nervous. You might feel you're losing control of what happens next. It's more like the opposite. You're taking power away from the kid who's been bullying you. You're saying, *"No, I'm not going along with this."*

Believe in yourself.
The bullying will stop eventually. Your life will get better—trust in that. For now, stay close to your friends and the grownups who protect you. Tell people what's happening, what you think, and how you feel. Speaking out will get you more support. It will also give you the strength that comes from finding your own voice.

forgiveness

Two years ago, this one girl bullied me horribly. Now she's nice to me. All my friends expect me to forgive her because "she's changed—she's so sweet now." But I can't. The memory haunts me. I can still see her sneer when she said that no one liked me and I should give up on life. I don't think I'll ever be able to forgive her or get over it. Is that wrong? —Bullied

No, it's not wrong. You know how you feel. You can't fake that away. And despite what your friends say, you don't owe this girl forgiveness or anything else. That said, something needs to change. The bullying is alive inside you when you're with your friends at school. You're still struggling with fear, shame, and anger. You deserve to be happier than this, and you can be.

Make it a goal: *I want to feel better*. Then start changing the channel when these dark memories come up. Instead of reliving a horrible moment, turn your mind to one that gave you joy. If your brain flips back to the bad stuff (it probably will), just take some slow, deep breaths and turn it around again. Tell yourself you're breaking a habit. Expressing your feelings can help, too. Write or paint them out. Talk to an older person, ideally a counselor.

Also, if you've never talked openly with the girl who haunts you, now might be the time. The point is not to attack her. The point is to talk about what happened. Ask: "Do you ever think about fifth grade? I do." She may be defensive, but she also might be ready to talk. What was going through her mind back then? Does she understand what it meant to you? Having some answers may help you, and having had the strength to bring this out of the shadows can help as well. Healing is a process of many steps, big and small. This can be one of them.

Everyone says that I'm so nice and so pretty and so caring, but when I look in the mirror I see an ugly, mean girl struggling with anger. I have been a jerk and a queen bee since third grade, and I hate myself. How can I turn around and be the nice, loving girl I was before? —Mean Girl

You don't need to go back to third grade. You just need to go back to being yourself. Apologizing is a good place to start. Who got hurt when you were being a "jerk"? Go to them and say you're sorry: "I've been thinking about how I behaved last year. I teased you all the time. It was mean. I know I hurt you, and I'm really sorry." Do what you can to repair the damage. If you told a lie, correct it. If you destroyed a friendship, go to the people involved and explain what you did.

The goal here is not forgiveness. Your victim might forgive you or she might not—that will be her choice. The goal is to make this other girl's life better. Chances are, she's been struggling with pain and anger every bit as much as you are. You want to free her from that.

Yet apologizing can help you, too. It helps because you are throwing off the fake "you" and doing something you know is right. You've stopped pretending to be perfectly pretty and nice. You've started being real.

You can like yourself for that, and maybe start forgiving yourself, too. You may have bullied somebody. That doesn't make you a bully for life. You have plenty of time to take what you've learned and become the person you want to be. It all starts with what you do next.

What if no one ever teased anyone about hair or clothes or family or anything else? What if we all thought about the impact of what we said before saying it? Then maybe the only place drama would exist is on the stage.

—Cierra

Quiz

casting call

Quiet backstage! The lights are going down. The curtain is rising. The show's about to begin. This time don't pick the part you *might* play. Pick the part you *want* to play.

Scene 1
Zoey and Aria have been fighting for three days straight, and you're in the middle.

a. You talk, text, talk, text, get angry, get sad, get confused, chat online, and lose sleep. Needless to say, your big presentation does not go well.

b. You tell Zoey and Aria that they should talk with each other directly and figure it out.

Scene 2
Yesterday you told Jaycee your secret. Now she's told it to Taylor.

a. You act like it's nothing, but inside you're thinking, *Just you wait, Jaycee. I'll get you back.* You know things about her, you know how to use them, and you will.

b. You find Jaycee and say, "I asked you not to tell anybody. You broke your promise. I'm mad. If you want to be friends, you can't do that to me again."

Scene 3
You're brooding about Ashley when your little sister throws herself on your bed. Notebooks go flying. Argh!

a. You yell at your sister and get grounded. Stuff like this happens to you *All. The. Time.* Life is unfair.

b. You stop and ask yourself, *Why am I so mad?* Talking through your feelings calms you down and helps you identify the real problem: Ashley. So after your sis helps pick up your stuff, you call your friend and say, "Can we talk?"

Scene 4

Sophia has decided she doesn't like Amber. Now she says you and your other friends should stop liking Amber, too.

a. What Sophia says goes. If she tells you to stop talking to Amber, you'll do it. If she wants to exclude Amber, OK. If she thinks you should make jokes about Amber, or whisper and spread stories about her— that's what you'll have to do. You're sorry for Amber, but there's no going against Sophia.

b. You tell Sophia no. She can't order you around. She shouldn't be ordering other people around either, and—by the way—it's wrong to mess with other people's relationships.

Scene 5

You're with your friends.

a. You feel fake.

b. You feel great!

Answer

Did you pick lots of **a's?** Didn't think so. Why would you? You want to be happy. You don't want drama to consume your life. You don't want conflicts in one part of your life to affect another, either. You want to be able to speak freely with your friends about how you feel. You want to speak up for what you deserve and to disagree when you have to. You want friendships based on affection—not on power, rules, and exclusion. And guess what? You can have them! You're ready to turn the page on drama and play the best role in the world: being you.

a fresh start

What would a world without drama look like?

Anna, Emma, and Grace signed up for the talent show together. They disagree about the song, but they'll figure it out.

Bianca broke up with Jason. She was sad, but Jasmine cheered her up.

Ava, Aaliyah, and Lila are volunteering once a week at a nursing home. Ava's mom drives them.

There's a new girl in school. She always wears purple. She taught Min-ju how to use a pottery wheel.

Katie's big clarinet solo is tonight. Maya sent her a text that said: "Go get 'em, KT. You rock! ♥"

Olivia's got Jackson doing yoga.

Rachel started a school newspaper. Mikayla's doing cartoons for it.

Nice!

Kids will always have problems. That's just part of being human. People will always make mistakes and do things they shouldn't do. But it's all ten times easier to handle without the drama. Conflicts don't blow up into full-force hurricanes. You can see what's really going on. Relationships are more relaxed, less fearful.

If you're knee-deep in drama at your own school, this vision of calm may seem a long way off. But cool down the drama that affects you directly, and your friends have a chance to do the same. You can build on that.

Try talking with your close friends about the drama you're seeing and experiencing. Use this book, if it helps. Take the quizzes together. Talk about similar issues in your own friendships. Discuss the **rewrite the script** pages. Are there ways to put some of those ideas to work in your own lives? How can you help one another do that?

Make a pact for how you'll treat one another, too. You won't always live up to your ideals, but if you keep trying you'll get better at it. Little by little, you'll be more open and honest. You will trust one another more. You'll give one another the strength and courage to be yourselves. And when you walk in the door at school, you'll bring all that with you. You may be surprised just how far those ripples can spread.

It can start with you. It can start now.